To Peter

an Italian
an Trying!

Happy Birthday!

Don, Louise,
+ Mike

HOW TO BE AN ITALIAN

HOW TO BE AN ITALIAN

BY LOU D'ANGELO

PRICE/STERN/SLOAN
Publishers, Inc., Los Angeles

Portions of this book originally appeared in the magazine, *Grump.*

The book's special photographs were posed
by a non-professional model,
Bruno Scordino.

Photography by Ardis Wade

Our thanks to Columbia Pictures for the photo of Miss Cardinale, to Embassy
Pictures for Mr. Mastroianni and to God for Miss Loren.

Eighth Printing — October, 1973

To Romulus and Remus,
who made it all possible.

CONTENTS

THE IMPORTANCE OF BEING ITALIAN

Some people achieve greatness; others have it thrust upon them. Then there are those people who are *born* Italian.

If you are not an Italian, don't be despondent. You can *become* an Italian. You can learn to look, dress, walk, gesticulate, think, and talk Italian by mastering a few simple rules. Think of the immediate advantages this will mean for you:

1. You won't have to read movie sub-titles.
2. You can talk back to your barber.
3. If you're an Italian man, you can pinch girls and be "simpatico." (If you're a Lithuanian man and pinch girls, you're a sex maniac.)
4. If you're an Italian girl, you won't have to wear a girdle, comb your hair, or shave under your arms. Not only will you be more sexy, you'll have more time to take advantage of it.
5. You'll be able to pronounce "Marcello Mastroianni," "minestrone" and "ciao."

6. You can become a popular or operatic singer (being Italian is not only important, it's a clause in the contract).
7. You'll have Columbus Day off.

The long term advantages of being Italian are even more impressive. In ascending order of importance:
1. You can be elected to the Mafia.
2. You can be elected Pope.
3. You can be invited to Frank Sinatra's house.

Take off your Italian sunglasses and look around. Jewish mothers, wearing Italian dresses and Italian shoes, are serving Pizza instead of chicken soup. Jack Valenti (an Italian from *Texas*) is boss of the movies. Ben Gazzara has stepped into Tab Hunter's shoes. Joseph Califano is a top presidential assistant. American millionaires and teenagers all want to drive a Ferrari or an Alfa-Romeo. What is the world's greatest tourist attraction? Rome!

Take another look. Have you ever seen a *queer* Italian? Of course not. Italian men are all irresistible to women. Unfortunately, all women are irresistible to Italian men, so that comes out even. But go to your neighborhood

Herman Dopelhoff, an unsuccessful CPA from Hoboken, N.J., who decided to become an Italian several years ago and is now a popular "In" person.

Bocce court and watch the old Italian men. Tough, strong, lively aren't they? They've had to be.

It's the same with Italian women. Sophia Loren, Virna Lisi, Gina Lollobrigida, Silvana Pampanini, Claudia Cardinale, and others too numerous to spell right, are more than sex *symbols*. They're the genuine article.

Italians are not only sexier, they're healthier. I've never met an Italian who worried about unsaturated fats.

Italians have achieved prominence in every field. They sing better, act better, cook better, build better and goof-off better. The Italian way of doing nothing sounds glamorous and exciting—*Dolce Far Niente*.

Fashion, food, furnishing, politics, production, and promotion — everything glamorous in today's world has an aura of tomato sauce and parmesan cheese. The handwriting is on the wall and it says: Viva Italia.

Miss Gertrude Svenson who was a skinny Swede until 1959 when she became an Italian. Altho she has never learned to sing, Miss Svenson has developed other Italian characteristics.

KNOW YOUR ITALIAN-AMERICAN HISTORY

Now that you've decided to become Italian, it is important that you know something about your ancestors who made this country great.

The first people who came to America were Italian. They were Cristoforo Colombo, Giovanni Cabotto, and Amerigo Vespucci. They were also the first Italians who changed their names for business reasons. Colombo changed it twice: first to Cristóbal Cólon, as a favor to Queen Isabella, later to Columbus, as a favor to Ohio. Cabotto became John Cabot. Those people in Massachusetts who talk only to God ought to be talking Genoese dialect.*

Of the three explorers, Vespucci took the oddest name of all—Americus Vespucius. He was rewarded by having the country named after him.

*If you don't believe this, look up John Cabot in any encyclopedia. And congratulations; healthy skepticism is an Italian trait worth developing.

Typical Non-Italian (Male)   *Typical Italian (Male)*

Thus, Italians infiltrated into this land under assumed names. Now that Italian supremacy is out in the open, there is no longer any need for an Italian to change his name, although many still do, particularly in show business. Reasons for this vary. One Italian changed his name to Jose Greco so he could become a great Spanish dancer. Others, such as Tony Bennett, Anne Bancroft, Frankie Laine, Jackie Vernon, Fabian, Vince Edwards and Dean Martin, probably changed them because their original names wouldn't fit on a marquee.

But since you who are reading this want to *become* Italian, the first thing to do is to choose yourself a genuine Italian name. Once you've established yourself, you can always change it back.

CHOOSING AN ITALIAN NAME

In the preceding chapter we learned that some Italians changed their names. But many more people have adopted Italian names, just as you are about to do, and become successful. Attila (who was a Hun) chose an Italian name. So did Truman Capote, Dondi, Geronimo and U Nu.

The easy way to let people know you have become an Italian is to call yourself "Tony," but if you want to be more elaborate a good place to look for a name is the libretto of the opera *Manon Lescaut** by Puccini. Under the credits you will see that it was written by Giacomo Puccini "with the aid of Domenico Oliva, Marco Praga, Giuseppe Giacosa, Luigi Illica and Giulio Ricordi."

Though all these first names are masculine, it's a simple matter to convert them if you are a woman or want a feminine first name for any other reason. Simply make the name end in "a": Giacoma, Domenica, Marca, Giuseppa, Luigia, Giulia.

In my own case I've had an Italian name since birth.

*Caution: Do not choose the name Manon Lescaut. It's French. There's no future in French names once you get past DeGaulle.

My parents were born in Sicily. Some Italians don't consider Sicilians proper Italians at all, but this is a Civil Rights matter which we'll consider in the next chapter. The name D'Angelo means "of" or "from the angel." Many Italian names mean things, a point to consider when you pick your name. Olivia, for instance, means olive and Ricordi means remembrance. I've known Italians whose names translated to Fat, Skinny, Rabbit and Chicken (Grasso, Magro, Coniglio and Gallina).

Nicknames

Italians love to pin nicknames on people. People so pinned are stuck for life. These nicknames are more graphic than complimentary. Typical ones are: Smelly Exhaler, Dyed Eyebrows, Mosquito Attractor, Mrs. Soft Stomach and Mr. Hairy Nostrils.

Beware of such a fate. You may have chosen an elegant Italian name from our list—say, Domenica Illica-Praga. But scratch your head once in the presence of a born Italian and you shall be known thenceforth and forever as Little Miss Itching Dandruff Scales.

Typical Non-Italian (Female)   *Typical Italian (Female)*

YOUR NEW HOME TOWN
IN THE OLD COUNTRY

Now that you've chosen a new Italian name, you should decide what part of Italy your family came from. Your fellow-Italians are bound to ask.

On a map, Italy looks as though it might have been designed by Capezio, the great Italian bootmaker. The boot is divided into seventeen regions. An eighteenth region, called Sicily, lies just off the toe and is kicked regularly.*

Each of the eighteen regions is divided into several provinces, but to simplify your choice, I suggest that we divide Italians into three very broad categories:

1. The Northern Italian
2. The Southern Italian
3. The Sicilian

*A nineteenth region, Sardinia, is many miles from the mainland, across the Tyrrhenian Sea. Sardinians, perhaps because of their isolation, don't seem to be participating in the mainstream of Italian success. We will ignore Sardinia.

The Northern Italian

If you are tall, blonde and blue-eyed, you need not resign yourself to lifetime servitude as a Swede. You too can be an Italian. Just decide to come from *L'alt'Italia*, that is, "High" or Northern Italy.

Northern Italians are continually being told, "Funny, you don't look Italian," and "If you're Italian, how come you're not eating ravioli, manicotta, pizza, lasagne, or anything with tomato sauce on it? As a matter of fact, what *is* that slop you're eating?"

The slop is *polenta*, an oatmeal-like mess which is to Northerners what pasta is to Southerners.

Northern Italians become captains of industry and leaders of finance. Some of them invent things. Marconi invented the radio, for instance, and Enrico Fermi put the mushroom in the atomic bomb.

If you decide to come from the North, you must look down on all Italians who come from south of Rome. As for yourself, you should preferably come from Milano (Milan), Torino (Turin), Firenze (Florence) or Bologna (the same in any language). Maybe Venezia (Venice). Most of Shakespeare's Italians came from Verona. They also came to a bad end, so forget it—it's a hard luck town.

As a Northern Italian, you should lose no opportunity to point out that *all* the great Italians—Dante, Leonardo, Michelangelo, Galileo, Rafaello, etc.,—were Northerners. Mussolini was a Southerner.

The Southern Italian

Most Italians in America are Southern Italians and most of them are Neapolitans. Naples is a sea port, and, according to Northerners and Sicilians, a den of thieves. Actually, the *Camorra*, the Neapolitan version of the Sicilian Mafia, compares with it the way a freshman class play compares with *My Fair Lady*.

Near Naples are the towns of Pompeii and Sorrento. It is not recommended that you claim either of them as your birthplace. Very few people managed to emigrate from Pompeii, and as for Sorrento, Italian singers will always be telling you to come back to it.

Singers, in fact, are Naples' real claim to fame, and Neapolitans claim them all—Caruso, Martinelli, Gigli, Schipa, Pinza, Robert Merrill, Jan Peerce, Elvis Preslino, Frankie Avalon and The Silver Masked Tenor.

In a land of large families, Neapolitans have the largest families of all. That's why there are so many Neapolitans in this country. What most Americans think of as Italian food, is really Neapolitan food, and the *Napolitani* enjoy it almost as much as Americans do.

If you decide to come from Naples, or from other Southern towns such as Bari, Cosenza, Potenza, or Reggio Calabria, lose no opportunity to point out that *all* the great Italians—Dante, Leonardo, Michelangelo, Galileo, Rafaello, etc.,—were Southerners.

Mussolini was a Northerner. So was Lucrezia Borgia.

The Sicilian

As a Sicilian-Italian-American, be prepared for cracks from non-Italians (out people) about the Mafia. The best way to handle this is to look at them fixedly. If they know anything at all, they will recognize this as the *mafioso* stare. If this doesn't work, try making a fist and sticking it in your mouth. (Not *their* mouth—Sicilians are basically non-violent at heart.) Or try hissing the words "Cosa Nostra," "Omerta," or "Valachi," through your teeth. If all else fails, kiss them on the cheek.

Sicilians are supposed to be short and swarthy. They usually aren't but J. Carroll Naish (an Irishman) is, and most people think he looks Sicilian.

What Sicilians can do better than anybody is Uphold Their Honor and Command Respect. Contrary to popular belief, Sicilians do not treat their women as second-class citizens. They treat them as aliens.

You should decide to come from Sicily only if you're the strong, silent type and can hold a grudge for the rest of your life.

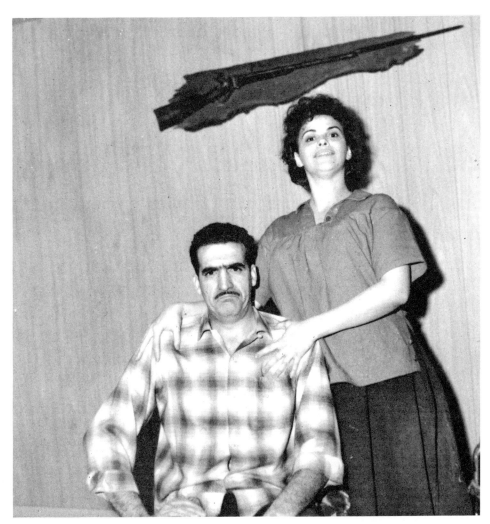

Typical Italian Couple

HOW TO LOOK ITALIAN

You may think that giving yourself olive oil shampoos and growing a mustache will help you look like an Italian man or woman, but the real secrets of the Italian Look are much more basic.

The Nose

All of us can't hope to achieve the nose greatness of such Italians as Dante, Jimmy Durante, Rocky Marciano, or Pinocchio. In fact, not every Italian has an acquiline, Roman or broken nose, but if you do, you're that much ahead of the game.

In other times, people have had "nose jobs" in the be-. lief that a nose like Doris Day's would make them look better. Whether it does or doesn't is open to argument, but, in any case, the object here is not to beautify ourselves but to win *Successo Italiano*.

You'll notice there's a lot of talk in Doris Day movies but no action.

Typical Italian Profile

33

If you want to give yourself an Italian looking nose fast, you may be able to find a cooperative doctor who has one left-over from an out-person's nose job. If not, there are a number of exercises you can perform.

1. Put your index finger to the tip of your nose and press down.
2. Visit an art museum, look at the pictures of Lorenzo de Medici, and think Nose.
3. Say something nasty to Frank Sinatra.

The last is the most painful way to Italianize your nose, but it's also the quickest.

The Eyes—Female

If you are a girl your eyes may be lined, framed in false lashes or naked — it doesn't matter. What is essential is that they look as though they had seen an indescribable amount of suffering. You too can achieve this Connie Francis Look.

Before you meet a man, prepare by peeling ten onions. Think about the time your goldfish died. When your escort arrives keep your eyes averted for at least five minutes. Stare sadly at a spot on the floor ten feet behind him.

Typical Italian Eyes, Female

Then suddenly move to within 18 inches, look directly at him and give him a knowing smile.

Repeat as often as necessary.

Male

Italian men should have deep shadows under their eyes (these are easy and fun to develop). They must say to a woman, "Ahh, the terrible dissipation I have known! Will you restore my faith in life, Signorina?"

An Italian man's eyes, like Superman's, must be able to look right through a woman. Start by looking at the tips of her shoes (or feet, if you are on the beach). Work your gaze up slowly, pausing in key places*, finally letting it rest on her forehead.

This technique shows her you are passionate, but also interested in her mind. Study Rossano Brazzi movies.

The Mouth

An Italian mouth can convey all sorts of things without ever uncovering a single tooth. In fact, an Italian can convey a myriad of different emotions with one simple expression. This basic mannerism of the mouth consists of

*If you're not sure which are the key places, you are not ready to become an Italian. Perhaps you could become an Albanian and then work your way up.

Typical Italian Eyes, Male

thrusting out the lower lip in a slight pout while keeping the upper rigidly vertical. In this way Italians denote bewilderment, annoyance, sympathy or lack of interest. Among many other things, this expression also says:

1. I don't know what you're talking about officer, I'm a legitimate businessman.
2. Okay, you want a crew cut, a crew cut is what you get.
3. No sister of mine is marrying a *Calabrese*.
4. Have it your way—Eleanora Rossi-Drago is a better actress than Maria Grazia Buccella.
5. I still can't figure out why Benito got mixed up with that German housepainter.
6. It could use a little more oregano.

You now have an Italian name, an Italian home town and an understanding of the first steps you must take in order to become an Instant Italian.

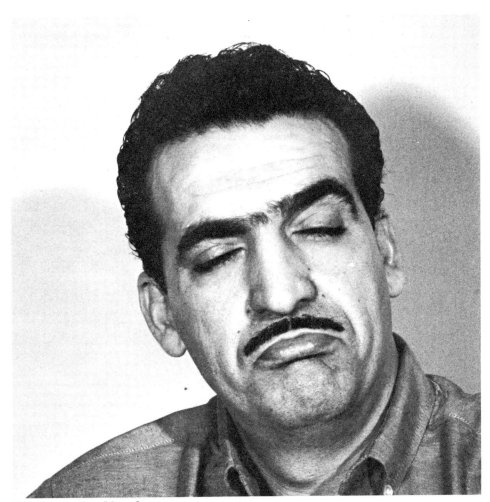

Typical Italian Mouth

HOW TO DRESS ITALIAN

In fashion, as everything else, Italian pre-eminence was established a long time ago. Just remember, the Italian dresses, Italian suits, Italian sweaters, Italian shoes, and Italian jewelry now worn by Americans, Britishers, and chic Lithuanians everywhere, were worn by Italians first.

A recent issue of *Harper's Bazaar* said that American women would soon be painting their legs purple. What a laugh! Italian lady grape-crushers have been doing it for years. And many of the same ladies were wearing boots around the house long before American girls adopted them to go out in.

Italian designers are now famous throughout the world. You can even get Pucci pants suits, Gino Paoli knitwear and Taverna shoes in Hong Kong. And the great Fontana makes more money fulfilling feminine dreams than the fountain named after her.

Such Italian designers for men as I. Magnani and Jean Casaneve are popular innovators. But even though it was

If you want to be taken for a well-to-do businessman or mafioso, keep the brim up, all around.

another Italian, Bronzini,who invented the necktie, Italian men have traditionally regarded this piece of apparel as an export item, preferring to wear their shirts open at the neck. The advantages are twofold: The chest hair peeking over the shirt is a surefire aphrodisiac to all women except Eskimos, and an open collar is more convenient for tucking in one's napkin. There was a time when the tucked-in napkin had replaced the red bandana which older Italian men used to wrap around their necks to absorb tomato sauce stains. But nowadays, the wide Mod neckties perform the same function more effectively since every splatter of *marinara* adds zest to the pattern. For this reason, you'll see more and more Italian men put on a necktie when it's time to eat.

The Mod tie, incidently, was not developed in England, but in Trapani province, Sicily, by Betta Rossi Modalino, a housewife and mother. She made the first one out of an old flowered tablecloth, after she got tired of her neighbors calling her *"L'Indiana"* just because her menfolk went around with red chests. Recently, *Signora* Modalino achieved another fashion first for her Mod males—the mini-tee-shirt. It is worn three inches above the navel.

The grey fedora snap-brim hat, which may or may not

Snap hat down in front if you prefer to be recognized as a show biz figure or sports hero.

Snap hat down on one side and up on the other if you'd rather be an artist, poet or opera singer.

Snap it down all around if your aim is to impersonate a member of the Italian royal family in exile.

be removed at the table, is the most indispensable symbol of male Italian affluence. Purchasing one will be one of the best investments you ever made. Just remember that styles may come and go, but in no case should the brim of your hat be less than two inches wide if you want to pass for a genuine Italian.

To round out your wardrobe you should also buy an Italian silk suit and Italian shoes.* Both should be one size too small.

These are available everywhere, but be sure not to accept substitute suits, since Italian manicotti-fed silkworms are far healthier than the sukiyaki-bred oriental ones, many weighing as much as 35 pounds. To insure the genuineness of your suit, look for the Union Label of the Amalgamated-Clothing-Workers-of-America-Now-Living-In-Retirement-In-Italy-On-Their-Social-Security.

If you are a woman, you are undoubtedly familiar with the range and excellence of Italian fashions. But if you prefer to save money, you can still pass for Italian. All you really need are pierced ears and a basic black apron.

*Better buy two pairs of shoes—one for the bocci court and another for everyday use.

WALKING ITALIAN STYLE

In Italy, taking a walk (*la passegiata*) is a well developed art, and one of the main forms of recreation. People walk from one end of a town square to the other and back again, watching each other closely. Nothing comparable exists in America outside of prison yards at recess, but you can still employ the techniques of Italian walking on your way to the supermarket, the bus or to school, and be recognized for the successful Italian you are.

Women

Never swing your arms walking. Fold them instead, as though you were clasping weighty secrets to your bosom. The only swinging should come from the hips. A daily second-helping of ravioli for dessert should make you an accomplished hip-swinger in no time. Keep your head high and your eyes lowered. This will help you avoid open manholes.

Men

Keep the head down, shoulders hunched, and hands in back pockets. Move from the knees, with a slight shuffling motion of your feet. Weave your head from side to side slightly. It isn't easy to synchronize all these movements. Practice is essential, since a less than perfect execution of the Italian male walk is liable to get you arrested for loitering. Study Marlon Brando in *On The Waterfront*. (If you don't know by now that Brando is an Italian name, you'd better start again with Lesson One.)

Children

Follow adult directions except when walking with parents. In that case, keep your guard up at all times.

ISOMETRIC COMMUNICATION

Now that you're looking reasonably Italian, and hence prosperous, attractive and important, it's time you learned to communicate Italian-style with your compatriates and fellow-leaders. This does not mean you're in for a lesson in spoken or written Italian. What we will take up first is the most important form of the language—Visual Italian.

Visual Italian can be expressed with a furrowed brow, inflated cheeks, raised eyebrows, drooping eyelids, a wrinkled nose, pursed lips, an outthrust chin, or shrugging shoulders—indeed with any part of the body, provided you're wearing open-toed shoes. But all other parts of the body combined do not equal in importance or approach the versatility and vocabulary range of Italian hands. Other parts are almost never moved in isolation but in conjunction with the hands. Hands are to Visual Italian what vocal cords are to the spoken language. As a matter of fact, even the vocal cords seldom operate independently. No Italian could speak at any length and keep his hands still. This explains why handcuffed Italians are notoriously uncommunicative.

But the opposite is not true, and Italians are perfectly able to talk with their hands when they can't use their voices. While Anglo-Saxons have reduced the function of the hand to that of a tape measure for horses, and hula dancers need grass skirts, ukeleles and guys singing in funny shirts for every movement of their hands to have a meaning all its own, two Italians can keep a lively conversation going for at least fifteen minutes and even get into an argument, with neither of them ever saying a word. Every Italian is a master of the art of Isometric Communication.

I had occasion to verify this recently, when, during a walk in my neighborhood (it's Italian, of course—the high rent district), I saw two men—one on the sidewalk and the other in a fifth floor window—greeting each other. The man on the street "spoke" first. He cupped his right hand, palm up, bunching his fingers and touching them together at the tips to the end of his thumb. By moving the hand slowly up and down from the wrist, he asked his friend: "What's new?" (Figure 1)

The man in the window answered by spreading the

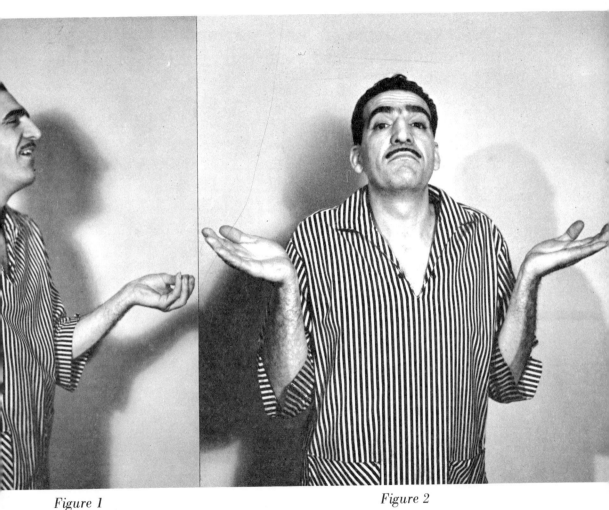

Figure 1

"What's new?"

Figure 2

"What should be new?"

fingers of both hands, also keeping his palms up. He moved his hands away from each other, turning them slightly upward and outward, thus signifying: "What should be new?" (Figure 2)

It must be noted that both men's movements could have meant a number of other things besides "What's new?" and "What should be new?" It all depends on who's doing the gesturing and the context in which it's being done. According to the circumstances and the place, the hand movement of the first man could also mean:

1. Okay smart guy, what are you doing with my wife?
2. What's the idea of kicking my bocci ball?
3. What's this I heard that Columbus was Jewish?
4. You call *this* spaghetti *al dente?*
5. Your daughter is getting to be quite a big girl.

The gesture of the second man could be used in response to every one of these questions, as follows:

1. Why are you making an exception in my case?
2. I saw you throw that spitter.
3. They said the same thing about LaGuardia.
4. What do you expect with a Puerto Rican cook?
5. If you ever come around here again, I'll kill you.

The language of Isometric Communication can be divided into three categories.

A. Those maneuvers requiring one or more, but less than five, fingers of one hand.

B. Those that make use of the whole hand or both hands.

C. Those that bring the hand into contact with another part of one's body.

The two gestures discussed thus far fall, of course, into category B. But mastery of all three categories is necessary if you are to achieve more than a childish level in expressing yourself. The most important thing to remember is to approach Isometric Communication with confidence and with your hands loose. To this end, a valuable exercise has been practiced for centuries by many Italians.

If you've ever been in an Italian neighborhood, you must have seen a group of people simultaneously sticking out some of their fingers at one another and shouting, "*Uno*," "*Due*," "*Tre*," "*Quattro*," "*Cinque*," "*Sei*," "*Sette*," "*Otto*," "*Nove*" or "*Dieci*." They were playing the game of *Morra*, the object of which is to call correctly the total number of extended fingers. There is no better way to develop manual Isometric dexterity and overcome stiffness. *Morra* also helps prevent the dreaded scourge that sometimes tragically robs an elderly Italian of the ability to communicate: arthritis of the hands. At the same time, you may win a few dollars.

The two men I saw must have been *Morra* champions, judging by the vigorous way in which they continued their conversation. The rest of that conversation will serve as a splendid lesson for your study.

For his next remark, the man on the street kept his right hand in approximately the same position as before — cupped, with fingertips touching his thumb. Only this time his wrist remained motionless, the only movement being a slight rubbing of thumb against fingers. (Figure 3). This gesture means only one thing in the Isometric vocabulary: money. The man in the window then cupped the four fingers of his right hand, and, keeping his thumb extended outward at right angles, touched the backs of them to the bottom of his chin and pushed out. (Figure 4).

Putting the two gestures together, I transcribed the following dialogue:

"Did you get the money?"

"No, the deal fell through."

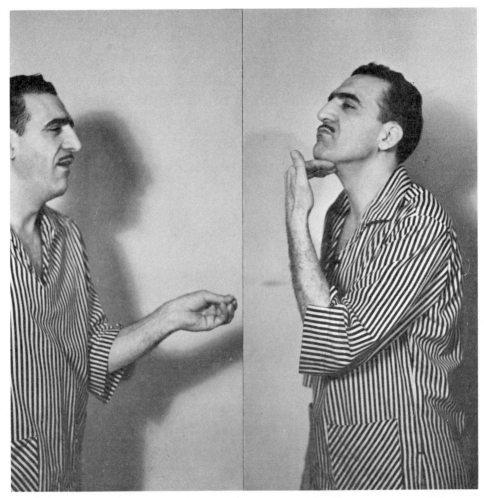

Figure 3   Figure 4

The second gesture could also have meant: "I have it, but you're not getting any," "You need a shave," or "I'm washing my hands and chin of the entire affair."

The man in the street seemed unconvinced. He extended his index finger and raised his thumb, almost the way children simulate a gun, but looser. He turned this hand clockwise, in a rapid, jerking motion, in the gesture meaning, "Nothing? You sure?" (Figure 5) For emphasis he could have performed the turning motion several times, in alternate directions.

The man in the window brought his hands together in an attitude of prayer and moved them vertically and rapidly from the wrist, several times in succession. (Figure 6) "What do you want from my poor life?" he was saying.

His friend was so angered by this brush-off, that he raised his right hand in a sweeping motion, describing an arc that started about at his waist, went out the length of his arm, and ended six inches over his head. (Figure 7) It was ballet-like in execution, but much more ominous in meaning: "You can go jump in Lake Como."

Furious at this insult, the man in the window made a fist of his fingers, holding his thumb straight out and stick-

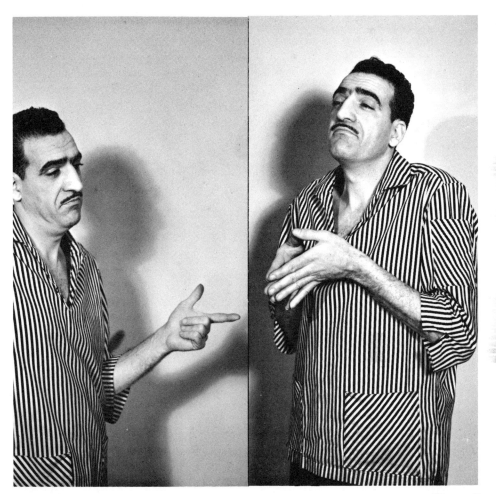

Figure 5   *Figure 6*

57

Figure 7   Figure 8

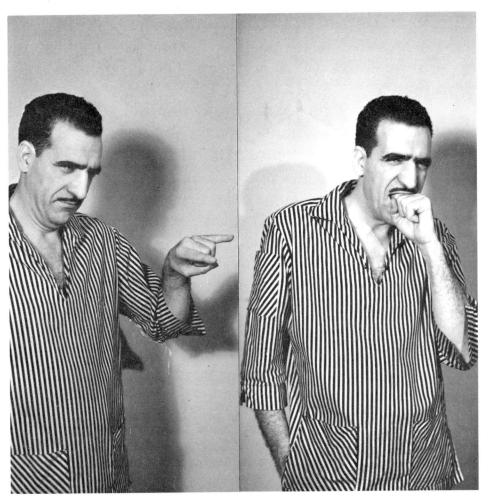

Figure 9   Figure 10

ing it in his mouth as though reverting to childhood. (Figure 8) Instead of sucking it, however, he bit it, and quickly expelled it by pushing against the back of his upper front teeth. (This gesture is not recommended for denture wearers.)

It was a dangerous warning of impending doom that should have sent the man on the street scurrying for cover had he not had the presence of mind to answer by extending the index finger and pinky of his right hand and waving them vigorously, keeping the two middle fingers under his thumb. (Figure 9) By this gesture, he single-handedly cancelled the threat and placed the man in the window under the spell of the evil eye. At this point, the latter man could have waved his index finger and pinky back, achieving a balance of terror, or he could have bitten the knuckles of his fist (Figure 10), thereby overwhelming the whammy's effectiveness by placing its sender under a new and even more ominous threat. But the conversation was growing so heated that I started biting my fingernails which means it's time to leave in any language.

You should master all the gestures described if you want to achieve Isometric Communication and don't want to be pushed around. In addition, you will find it helpful to practice these simple, often-used phrases:

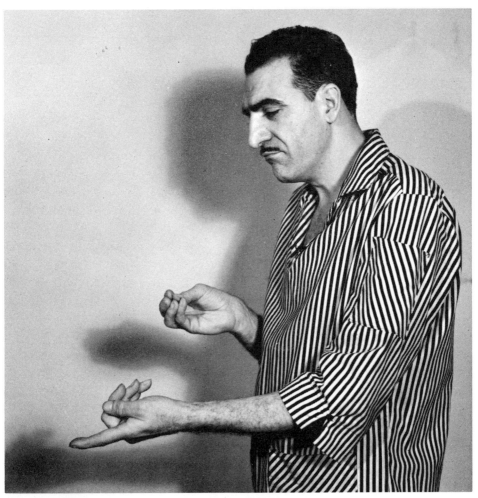

"How much?"
From the Italian: Quanto costa?

61

"Too much!"
Ital: Troppo!!!!!

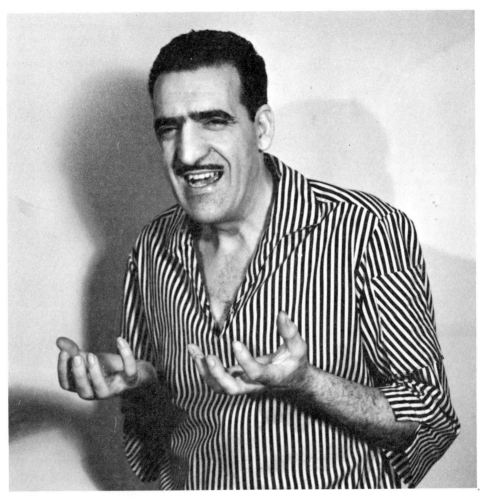

"Good afternoon, Miss."
Ital: Va-va-voom!

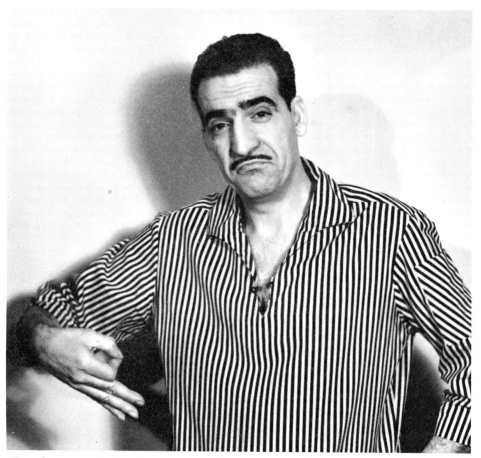

(Forefinger and thumb are pressed together and drawn horizontally across the body.)
"No sweat."
Ital: Itsa hokay, Keed.

(Forefinger and thumb pinch and twist.)
"That young lady is obviously a person of great refinement, good breeding and superior intelligence. If I were not a loyal husband and the father of eleven children I might be tempted to invite her to share a Mozzarella Custard with me."
Ital: Va-va-va-va-va-va-va-Voom!!!

I agree that Fellini is a good director, but somehow the philosophical basis
of this particular cinema escapes me.''
Ital: Che brutta puzza!

THE KAMA PIZZA

You can't expect to pass for a natural-born Italian unless you are prepared to excel at everything a natural-born Italian excels at, namely, everything. And bear in mind that to many Italians, sex is everything.*

Oddly enough, the sexual eminence represented by such ancient Romans as Ovid (the Henry Miller of his day) and Messalina (a lady who once took on an entire Roman legion while nibbling grapes before breakfast) seemed to fade with the empire, and it took Italians a long time to re-acquire mastery in lovemaking. Once they did, however, there was no holding them back.

The First Great Italian Lover

Giovanni Casanova, who was born in Venice in 1725, spent a rich, full life in Rome, Naples, Florence, Corfu, Constantinople, Paris, the south of France, Holland, Germany, Switzerland, Russia, Poland, Spain, Bohemia,

*In Italian, sex is a five letter word, sesso, which is used only in the sense of gender, as in il sesso debole, the weaker sex. There is no word for sex in the sense we're using it here. But if you have any sense at all, you already know that in Italian, actions speak louder than words.

and other places, most of which he was thrown out of. Everywhere he went, women fainted and strong men wept. Even if he hadn't been so fond of garlic sauce, Casanova's effect would doubtless have been the same. He was the great pioneer who extended the boundaries of Italian supremacy to include the province of the heart, and, due to his eating habits, heartburn.

Before Casanova's time, Italians had made out fine, except in making out. Leonardo DaVinci and Michelangelo, for instance, ignored *signorine* altogether, and Dante, who'd had eyes only for Beatrice Portinari since he'd been nine years old, had one hell of a time.

Italian women fared little better in those unhappy days between the fall of the Roman Empire and the rise of Casanova. True, Lucrezia Borgia attracted quite a few husbands and boy friends, but, having attracted them, she had no idea what to do next, except mix them a drink the way she'd seen her relatives do. She used the same expression they did, too: "Name your poison." Unfortunately for her romantic fulfillment, Lucrezia was a very literal-minded person. It was left up to Casanova to formulate the principles and establish the image of the great Italian lover. You can read all about it in his *Memoirs*, the Supreme Court being what it is today.

Sal Mineo's Secrets

Casanova's name became synonymous with "lover-man" all over Europe. Two centuries later, another Italian's name acquired the same definition in the New World. Unlike his illustrious predecessor, Valentino did not need personal contact with a woman in order to seduce her. He did it from a distance and without uttering a sound. While employing the basic expressive technique described in Chapter Five, he brought new dimensions to the range of Italian romantic expression that have served Italian lovers on-screen and off, ever since: the dilation of the nostrils and breathing through the mouth. The next time they show a Valentino movie on the Late Late Late Show, keep your eyes open, if you can. And your mouth.

These methods have been brought to a peak of perfection in our own day by Valentino's successor, Sal Mineo. The next time you see him, watch his nostrils. Flared, aren't they? Now look at his mouth. When you pay a couple of thousand dollars to have your teeth capped, you want people to *see* them.

The Kama Pizza Heavy Breathing Exercises

Before attempting nostril dilation, nose hairs should be trimmed and all nasal passages cleared. A product like Dristan, used according to the manufacturer's directions, may be helpful in achieving the latter. If you are Jewish, you know the effectiveness of horseradish, but a more Italian way to do it is to inhale cheese fumes daily. *Romano, Pecorino,* and *Caciocavallo* cheeses are excellent for this purpose. Moving next door to a *Latticini* store, an establishment where Italian dairy products are sold, is recommended.

When you have taken care of these preliminaries, begin your exercises by flaring both nostrils together fifteen times. Then flare the left nostril only, fifteen times again. I know, it's not easy. Vittorio Gassman took years to master it. Rosanna Schiaffino was ready to throw in the handkerchief before she got it right. Courage.

Try the right nostril now, fifteen times. If you just can't do it, try opening a window or dabbing two or three drops of olive oil on the tip of your nose. When you succeed in attracting a fly to it, you should be able

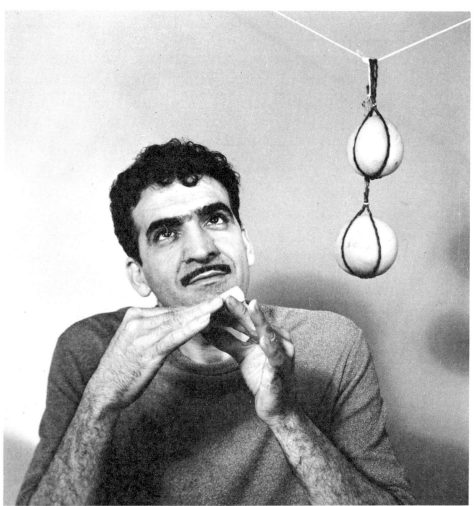

Proper Inhalation Practice, Cheese Fumes (p. 70)

to flare your nostrils with very little effort. Just be careful breathing in.

The simplest way to practice mouth-breathing is to pretend you are being examined by a doctor who is telling you to breathe deeply. Do this slowly and regularly for five minutes.

This simulated adenoidal condition is guaranteed to reduce American women of all ages to quivering lumps ready to be kneaded. Women, too, can use the technique on men with devastating effect. Not everyone is lucky enough to be born with big adenoids, though. Remember that the rest of us have to engage in constant practice.

Flattery Will Get You Everywhere

What separates the men from the boys—in other words, what separates Italian lovers from those of other nationalities—is the things they lie about. The American man, for instance, in trying to impress a woman, lies about *himself*—exaggerating or inventing his financial status, the importance of his job, his sufferings, even his previous amatory affairs. The Italian man, on the other hand, knows that the best way to impress a woman is to lie about *her*. He tells her she is the most beautiful, desirable, intelligent, and exciting creature he's ever met. This is done in accordance with the fine old Italian proverb: "You can catch more bunnies with snake-oil made from vine-ripened olives than you can with stale *prosciutto*."

Practice these sure-fire compliments in front of a mirror, checking constantly to see that your eyes, nose, and mouth are in the proper working order described in chapter 5:

1. "*Signorina*, your eyes are as liquid as *anisette*; your little ears remind me of chilled *marsala*; your lips are like *asti spumanti*. I am drunk with your beauty."

2. "Of course, to a woman of the world like yourself, what I've just said about the Blue Grotto at Capri must sound like child's play at Coney Island."

3. "On a diet, you say? But this is impossible, my gazelle! It is simply that you have a large frame— what we call in my country, '*la grande bellissima*'." (There is no such phrase, of course, but it gets the

zoftig ones every time, even if they understand Italian.)

Preliminary Petting, or: Antipasto to Amore:

Before attempting to get too physical, it is imperative that you enflame your loved one's ardor by making use of one or more of the following warm-up methods:

A. *Pinching*
This is to the *Kama Pizza* what scratching was to the *Kama Sutra*. It is, in fact, an even more refined act than the ancient Hindu one, and an entire book could be written on this subject alone. We will confine ourselves here to three fundamental pinches. A small helium-filled balloon will prove handy for practice sessions.

1. *The Pizzicato:* a quick, tweaking pinch performed with the thumb and middle finger. Recommended for beginners.

2. *The Vivace:* a more vigorous, multi-fingered pinch performed several times in rapid succession.

3. *The Sostenuto:* a prolonged, rather heavy-

Proper Pinching Practice, Kama Pizza (p. 74)

handed, rotating pinch for use on "living girdles."

B. *Kissing*

You have already learned that an Italian can express a myriad of emotions without opening his mouth. When it comes to kissing, however, the wider he can open it, the better. Referring to open-mouthed osculation as "French kissing" (a mistake some out-people still make) dates from the Bourbon conquest of Italy. Happily, most people now realize that Italians not only invented so-called "French kissing," they did it in 28 different flavors, not just Bourbon.

As with pinching, it will be impossible here to launch into an exhaustive study of Italian kissing.* It will be enough for our purposes to clarify the differences among the main categories, geographically.

1. *The Northern Italian Kiss:* Northern Italians kiss with a great deal of vigorous tongue flicking, a characteristic probably evolved from their habit of kissing ladies' hands in the days

*You are, of course, encouraged to pursue these studies on your own, if you don't mind getting exhausted.

when Northern Italian ladies did their own baking.

2. *The Southern Italian Kiss:* a wet, extremely passionate kiss that can get pretty sloppy, since Neapolitans never stop singing "O Sole Mio." For this reason, this is sometimes called a "sole kiss."

3. *The Sicilian Kiss:* Sicilians kiss more thoughtfully than other Italians. This is so because they must be careful what part of the other person's face they kiss. An inch or two either way can mean the difference between "I love you," and a renewal of the Hundred Years War.

The Positions

When you are ready for the main event, you may employ any of the following embraces. Study them carefully beforehand; no written explanation is necessary.

Position 54*: The Half-Valentino with full Janet Gaynor
Position 55: The Flying Marinara

*If, after getting this far, you can't ad-lib the first 53 positions, you are definitely an under-achiever. Apply for remedial assistance at your local Vittorio DeSica fan club.

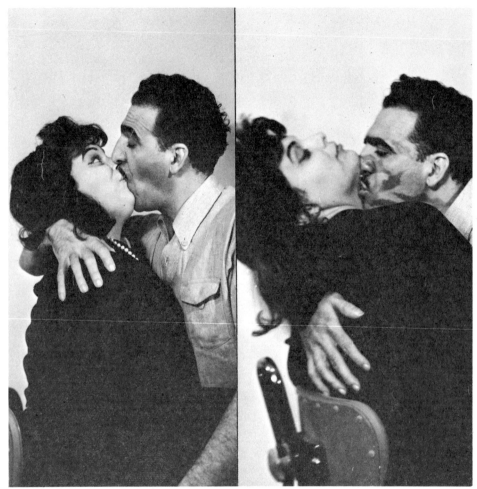

Northern Italian Kiss   *Southern Italian Kiss*

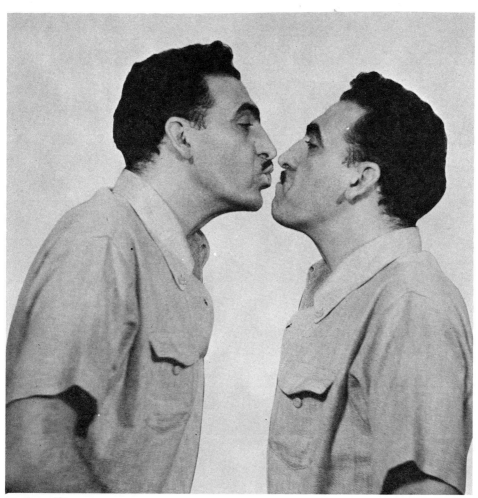

Sicilian Kiss

Position 56: The Double-Brazzi Wristlock
Position 57: The Sinatra Spin
Position 58 through 142: Repeat as above, this time indoors.

If All Else Fails

If you have failed in attracting a loved one by the fore-going means, try this time-tested Italian aphrodisiac.

1½ quarts boiling water	1 oz. grated Parmesan cheese
¼ lb. noodles	1 tbs. butter
½ chopped onion	1½ stalks diced celery
½ clove minced garlic	1 large diced potato
1 cup finely cut string beans	½ cup fresh peas
1 tbs. olive oil	½ tsp. chopped parsley

salt and pepper to taste

Cook onion and garlic in oil and butter about 2½ minutes or until slightly brown. Add celery and the potato. Cook for 10 minutes in covered pot. Add the boiling water. Cook 15 minutes more. Add string beans, peas, noodles, salt and pepper, and cook slowly for 20 minutes. Sprinkle with parsley and cheese. Drink it all down while it's still very hot. Congratulations: you have just consumed four servings of minestrone. What more do you want? Sex?

Marriage

Even if you've followed all the instructions so far without success, *you have not failed!* Though you may be unlucky in love, you can still *marry* an Italian. All you need is the plane or boat fare to Italy. For the fact is that while Italians are supreme all over the world, Italians in Italy look up to Italian-Americans as the greatest *paisani* of them all. You will receive a hero's welcome and dozens of marriage proposals. You won't receive the proposals directly, of course, but the parents of your prospective mate will let you know in no uncertain terms that you have a friend in *Reggio Calabria.*

When you go to Italy with marriage in mind, it is recommended that you stay away from the main tourist centers and concentrate your activities in the smaller towns of the South and in Sicily. You have an advantage if you are a man, since these places have a surplus of unmarried women.

But girls stand a good chance, too, particularly if they're not bashful about flashing their money around.

Just make sure you flash enough of it so your future husband's relatives can see you're able to pay *their* fare over to America, too.

Family Planning

Plan on having a large one.

Bringing Up Bambini

Sooner or later, every Italian parent must come to grips with the problem of sex education. Adequate sex education is of the utmost importance if you want your child to grow up as a well-adjusted Italian. When he or she starts asking those ticklish questions, the Italian mother must not blush or fumble for words: she must face facts. She should give her kid a slap across the mouth and say, "That's just a love tap. When your father comes home, you're really gonna get it." If, on the other hand, these questions are asked of the father, he should say, "What are you asking me that for? Don't you know that kind of stuff can make you crazy? Why don't you go play in the street?" Then he should give the kid a slap across the mouth and say, "It's a good thing you didn't ask your mother that."

Usually, these tactics are enough to solve the problem

Typical Italian Bambino

of Italian sex education. Occasionally, however, a tough, stubborn kid will keep on asking no matter how hard he's hit. In these cases, it is best to give him some kind of an answer.

Accordingly, here are the most commonly asked questions, and the approved responses.

Q. Where do babies come from?
A. From the outskirts of Palermo.

Q. Why do I have a belly button?
A. They were out of belly zippers.

Q. Does it hurt to have a baby?
A. You ever try having one and boy, is it gonna hurt! I'll knock your teeth out.

Q. Why is Pasquale's mommy getting so big?
A. I hear she spreads *mozzarella* on her Metrecal cookies.

Q. What is birth control?
A. That's enough now, I'll break your head!

HOW TO BE AN ITALIAN
IN YOUR SPARE TIME

Just as there are people who spend their week at a regular job wearing conservative clothes, and then go out on weekends wearing sandals, flowers in their hair, and carrying bongos hoping they'll pass as Bohemians, so, too, there are part-time Italians.

If you have decided that being an Italian the year 'round would be too much of a strain (you may own a Chinese laundry, for instance, or be a career Army officer), you might wish to consider becoming a part-time Italian. If you do, you've got to be extra diligent in your studies. There is nothing more ludicrous than the sight of a weekend Italian waving his arms about aimlessly and wearing buttons which say "Italian Power" or even "Kiss me, I'm Italian." This fools nobody. Real Italians will revile and despise you, as well they should. No Italian needs buttons to have power or to have people kiss him. Italian power is something that comes from deep inside, like a rumbling in the stomach.

Ditto Italian sex appeal. Nor should you delude yourself that it is enough to take Italian LSD (Lasagne, Scungilli, and Ditalini) with your meals. No, being even a part-time Italian is a full-time job. So go back to the beginning of this book, do the exercises, arrange your face, flex your fingers, put on the proper clothes, and *think* Italian. Actually, by merely standing on a street corner and practicing all you've learned, you should attract a crowd in no time. Or you can frequent the popular "in" places where successful Italians congregate: Tiffany's, the Stock Exchange, Appalachin. But, if you require further assistance, consider these crash methods:

Men:

The next time you attend an Italian movie, wait in back until your eyes get adjusted to the light. Then look over the auditorium, choose a seat beside a likely prospect, and, when a particularly silly sub-title appears on the screen, something like: "What's happened to us, Ruggiero? What went wrong?" laugh uproariously. When your pretty neighbor turns to look at you quizzically, say in a confidential tone, "Ah, *signorina*, they leave out so much in the translation."

Never order spaghetti in Italian restaurants; order

spaghettini, with tomato sauce on the side. When it arrives, take a few strands of the *pasta* in your right hand, hold them high over your upturned head and suck them noisily into your mouth. This is a fine old Italian tradition which is bound to win your waiter's respect, and attract the rapt attention of other diners, particularly that of some finicky female—the kind who could use a guy like you to straighten her out. Send a bottle of chianti over to her table.

Women:

In a butcher shop, point to the veal shanks and ask, "How much for the *ossi buchi?*" Not all butchers are Ernest Borgnine, but they all make good money.

Don't miss the Columbus Day Parade. Station yourself in or near the reviewing stand, or at least on the right hand side of the street, so that when the marchers turn "eyes right" they'll get a good view of you. Your reactions must be instantaneous when they do. Flare your nostrils, take a deep breath through your mouth and shout, "Down with Lief Ericson!" You can have your pick of the marchers.

FINAL EXAM

To assess how well you have learned your lessons, you should now complete this test, not referring back to the text of the book until you're finished. You're on your honor, so remember: an Italian's honor is his most precious possession. We have ways of dealing with sneaks.

1. America was discovered by:
   (a) Cristoforo Colombo   (b) Cristobal Colon
   (c) Christopher Columbus   (d) All three
   (e) George Washington

2. This man:

(a) didn't brush with Crest   (b) is in his second childhood   (c) hates your guts   (d) has a booboo on his wittle finger

3. If you had a "Mastroianni" you would:
   (a) serve it for the soup course   (b) see a doctor
   (c) keep it out of sight   (d) be Joseph E. Levine

4. Which of the following world-famous athletes does *not* have an Italian name:
   (a) Rocky Marciano   (b) Leonid Zhabotinsky
   (c) Eddie Arcaro   (d) Joe Pepitone   (e) Andy Robustelli

5. Which of the following creatures has the best memory:
   (a) a salmon   (b) a Sicilian   (c) an elephant
   (d) a Sicilian elephant

6. These people are:

   (a) married   (b) fooling around   (c) committing aggravated assault   (d) members of the Italian Parliament

7. Rudolph Valentino is best remembered by:
(a) Jose Greco   (b) senior citizens   (c) mouth breathers   (d) The Woman in Black

8. Every Sicilian is a legitimate businessman:
(a) true   (b) false   (c) maybe   (d) don't know
(e) it's nobody's business   (f) refuse to answer on ground of self incrimination

9. Every Italian child should know:
(a) about the birds and bees   (b) the truth about Neapolitans   (c) to keep his mouth shut   (d) the Anthony Franciosa Story

10. Complete this sentence in 2,500 words or more:

"Becoming an Italian has made me a superior person because..."

All the answers have been stated or implied in the preceding chapters. Score 10 points for each correct answer. A score of 80 to 100 indicates that you can pass for Italian with ease and are eligible for membership in the American-Italian Anti-Defamation League. *Congratulations!*

50 to 70 points means you are likely to be taken for an Italian most of the time, particularly in Bulgarian neighborhoods.

With a score of 20 to 40 points, you'll have to limit yourself strictly to low-starch spaghetti.

If you scored 10 points or zero, you flunk and ought to be ashamed of yourself. Or, as your Italian superiors would say: ⫸→

PUBLISHED BY

PRICE
STERN
SLOAN